Project Management

A Compact Guide to the Complex World of Project Management

By Jefferson Hanley

First Edition, 2015

Table Of Contents

Legal Notice:

This book is copyright protected. This is only for personal use. You cannot amend, distribute, sell, use, quote or paraphrase any part or the content within this book.

Disclaimer Notice:

Please note the information contained within this document is for educational purposes only.

Every attempt has been made to provide accurate, up to date and reliable complete information no warranties of any kind are expressed or implied. Readers acknowledge that the author is not engaging in rendering legal, financial or professional advice.

without the consent of the author or copyright owner. Legal action will be pursued if this is breached.

By reading any document, the reader agrees that under no circumstances are we responsible for any losses, direct or indirect, which are incurred as a result of use of the information contained within this document, including – but not limited to errors, omissions, or inaccuracies.

SECTION I

Project Management - An Essential Resource is a book unique unto itself. It has been written with a broad set of audiences in mind. As someone interested in project management, you will find that the contents of this book won't fit the typical mould of a project management text book - one that contains quizzes, exercises and refresher notes. Neither will you find that the book dedicates itself purely to the "real-world" experiences of project management professionals.

Instead, I have used a middle ground approach to organize the contents of the book, thereby appealing to the senses of both theoretical as well as practical-minded readers. I believe this unique approach to the book will not only help those readers who want a more subjective view of the project management world; but will also aid those new to the field gain valuable insight into projects and project management through the eyes of hands-on project manager experiences.

PREAMBLE

The body of knowledge, known as Project Management, is indeed extensive. And this enormity is sometimes the cause for aspiring project managers to shy away from embracing its best practices. Through my personal experiences, I've seen how projects that do not follow a disciplined methodology end up - as abysmal failures!

It is with that in mind that I decided to put together this book, as a means of encouraging managers, within a project setting, to adopt formal practices when managing projects. The way the book has been structured; line managers and project management practitioners can quickly learn the basics of formal project management, and start putting that knowledge into immediate practice.

OBJECTIVES OF THIS BOOK

There is indeed a lot of literature on Project Management. In fact, some might argue that project management is probably one of the most written-about subjects. However, through my personal experiences, and while conducting research on this and other books, I realized that there was a dearth of "compact" and "concise" information about project management. One of the objectives of this book is to remedy that situation!

As I noted in the Preamble to this book therefore, the objectives of this book are to:

a) Provide some academic background about Project Management to the reader

b) Deliver some strong principles of Project Management that are grounded in the Project Management Book Of Knowledge (PMBOK)

c) Provide lots of "real world" experience about what PMs will really face out there in the workforce

But the contents of this book go beyond that. This book can form an 'essential resource' for new entrants into the Project Management field, and can also serve as an invaluable resource for those PMs who don't have any "formal" project management training/knowledge, but want to acquire some "on the fly". So whether you are a novice PM, or a veteran, you are bound to find something of interest between the covers of this book.

WHO SHOULD READ THIS BOOK

As I indicated in the introduction to Section I, I wanted to make this book relevant to a broad segment of project management professionals - not just a select few. With that in mind, I carefully reviewed a vast body of project management knowledge, and selected topics of interest to readers:

- who are new to the management world, and are interested in knowing what Project Management is about
- that are already PMs and are thinking of acquiring formal PMI qualifications
- and veteran PMs who just want a sense of what other PMs (i.e. the Author) have experienced in "real world" Project Management

If you find yourself identifying with any of these groups of individuals, you'll find the contents of this book invaluable.

Happy reading...and I wish you a successful project management experience!

SECTION II

In this section of the book, we will explore the theoretical aspects of Project Management. Our discussions will primarily focus around the Project Management Body Of Knowledge (PMBOK), which is the industry accepted collection of all knowledge related to the art and science of managing projects.

1.0 INTRODUCTION

This chapter will introduce you to the world of project management by talking about what a "project" is. We'll start out by first exploring the main characteristics of projects, and how they differ from "business as usual" activity. Then, we'll discuss what project management is all about, and introduce you to the Project Manager (PM), and the constraining environment that he/she operates in.

We'll wind up our discussions by introducing you to the Project Management Office (PMO), a central hub through which all the project management activity is supported.

1.1 What is a Project?

In everyday life, we use the term "project" very often. You'll hear people say *"I have a weekend project"*, or *"I'm busy with my school project"*, or *"My wife has given me a project to deal with"* etc. And to a large extent, all of these activities might well be "projects" - loosely speaking. However, strictly speaking (from a business world point of view), these aren't considered "projects".

So what does one have to see in a particular activity, in order for it to be classified as a "Project"?

1.1.1   Temporary nature

When we define projects, they are there for a temporary duration. The term "temporary" does not, however, mean a short duration. On the contrary, many projects (like NASA's space shuttle project) last decades. When we look at "temporary" in the context of a project framework, we are looking at activity that:

- has defined timelines - start and end dates
- will cease once the project's objectives are reached
- will no longer be performed if it is determined that they do not further the projects' objectives

Often, this "temporary" characteristic of a project is determined by external market forces, such as a time-limited window of opportunity, or a deliverable-driven deadline, or the limited-availability nature of project resources. In that context then, an endeavour that goes on (indefinitely) cannot be classified as a project. So, if your wife/spouse assigns you the responsibility to lock the garage door every day before you leave home, that is not a "project". Why? Because it doesn't have a defined end date! But, if you were overseeing the installation of a new garage door this weekend, it would certainly be classified as a project.

1.1.2   Uniqueness

Activities that result in the creation of a unique product, service or capability (i.e. enabling the project sponsor to deliver new products or services) come under the purview of projects. Repetitive activity, such as producing batches of doughnuts each day, or inspecting and repairing mile after mile of train tracks on a daily basis will, however, not classify as a project.

Let's look at one of the every-day life examples from above. If the doughnuts produced in the above example were part of the ongoing service of the doughnut shop, it would not be a project. However, if the doughnuts were being produced with a new flavor, different design or other unique traits, then until those doughnuts were "here to stay", everything related to their design, production and introduction into the market would be a project unto itself.

1.1.3   Progressive Buildup/conclusion

Projects are characterized by a gradual and incremental clarification of what's needed to be done to complete them - i.e. the Scope of Work. The act of bagging groceries cannot be called a project, but the act of designing a new grocery check-out lane would most certainly fit within the classification of a project.

Why? Because the grocery store owner will initially have no idea what the new lane will look like. The project team will likely study shopper's habits, traffic patterns and other such criteria, to gradually build the scope of work for the new check-out lane project. By the time the lane is commissioned (i.e. the project concludes), it could end up being a fast lane, a lane for produce only, a lane that handles over-flow traffic only, or one that only serves senior (aged) shoppers.

The check-out-lane project team progressively defined the final deliverable. "Progressive buildup" doesn't mean the project team doesn't have a clue what they are doing, and ultimately end up producing something beyond the initial intent of the project. That's "scope creep" (more on that later). Progressive buildup is a deliberate act of refining the needs such that, by the end of the project, the sponsor gets exactly what he/she envisioned out of the project.

1.1.4   Different from "operational" activity

Projects must be differentiated from routine operational activity. In our discussions above, operating the doughnut shop on a day-to-day basis, or checking out customers once the new check-out lane is active, are examples of "business as usual" activities. Therefore, any activities that must be performed to maintain existing operations do not classify as project activity.

1.2   What is Project Management?

Well great! Now we know what a Project is, and we know what one is NOT too. So what's the buzz around "Project Management"?

Project Management is nothing more than "managing" a project. It's that simple! However, simply (and randomly) assigning work to a team, in the hope that something good happens, does not define the act of "management". Project Management requires the **deliberate** application of:

- proven knowledge
- effective tools, and
- successful techniques

in order to ensure that work on the project is conducted. The underlined word here is "deliberate". If random actions lead to spectacular success, despite the favorable outcome, it is not project management!

Let's take a closer look at what Project Management means by introducing ourselves to the Project Manager (PM).

1.2.1 The Project Manager

Simply stated, the Project Manager (PM) is the person responsible for the project management activities on any given project. It's that simple...and that complex!

More specifically, while he/she might not actually "work in the trenches" (though many of them do!), the PM's role (at a very high-level) includes:

- identifying project requirements
- defining project objectives
- producing project plans
- obtaining project resources (people, money, skills, tools/technology etc)
- ensuring the quality and timeliness of project activities
- communicating with all parties-at-interest in the project
- managing stakeholder expectations

Despite all the complex tasks entrusted to them, PM's are definitely no "Superheroes". They are mere mortals, with lots of flare and faults like you and I.

Encouraging random actions, unplanned activity or work assigned without regard to a proven framework or process, is not something that defines a Project Manager.

SOURCE: http://www.wiziq.com/

1.2.2 Project Management Constraints

So, from everything that we have discussed so far, it seems like becoming a Project Manager means living a pretty exciting life. Well, you could say that - if you are inclined towards some acrobatics and jugglery!

I say that because PM's work within a strict set of constraints that they continually have to juggle and balance, in order to deliver an ideal outcome from the project. In essence, the PM's world is focused around what's called the "triple constraints" of:

- **Schedule:** Which defines the project's time, including the duration it takes to perform individual tasks, as well as that taken for delivering unique milestones and, ultimately, the entire project

- **Cost:** Which refers to the budgetary challenges he/she needs to face when paying for project teams, materials, tools and supplies, as well as any required externally contracted resources

SOURCE: http://newproductvisions.com

- **Performance:** Which determines the scope of deliverables, their quality and the suitability of those deliverables to meet the overall objectives of the project

Given that all these three constraints must be balanced against the risks that the project faces, definitely makes the PM's life all the more interesting for sure! For instance, compromising on cost (lower cost resources), could have a direct impact on quality (performance). And trying to expedite timelines (schedule) may mean the PM needs more resources (cost) than he/she has.

1.2.3   The Project Management Office (PMO)

So, does the PM have to deal with all that stress all alone? Not entirely! In many organizations, especially where the project is large and complex, or organizations that are project-oriented (doing lots of projects), help comes by way of a Project Management Office (PMO). Essentially, the PMO is the central hub through which the PM can plan, coordinate and execute the entire project, while also receiving administrative support for the project team.

PMOs don't always have to be glass rooms, with long tables surrounded by Gant charts (project plans) plastered across walls. However, they do need to be established with PMO staff that is formally designated for the roles they need to play. In small project environments (2 to 3 member teams), a PMO might not be very effective. However, when multiple teams are working together, on multiple simultaneous projects, across functional boundaries and geographic borders, then that's where a PMO can truly be effective.

2.0 OVERVIEW OF THE PROJECT MANAGEMENT FRAMEWORK

For any body of knowledge to be credible and effective, it must function within the confines of a strong and robust framework, and Project Management is no different. The Project Management framework is a fusion of two key elements for managing projects:

- A project lifecycle, which governs various stages of a project, from Initiation to Closeout; and
- A set of project management processes, mapped into Process Groups, which must be adhered to when managing each stage of the lifecycle

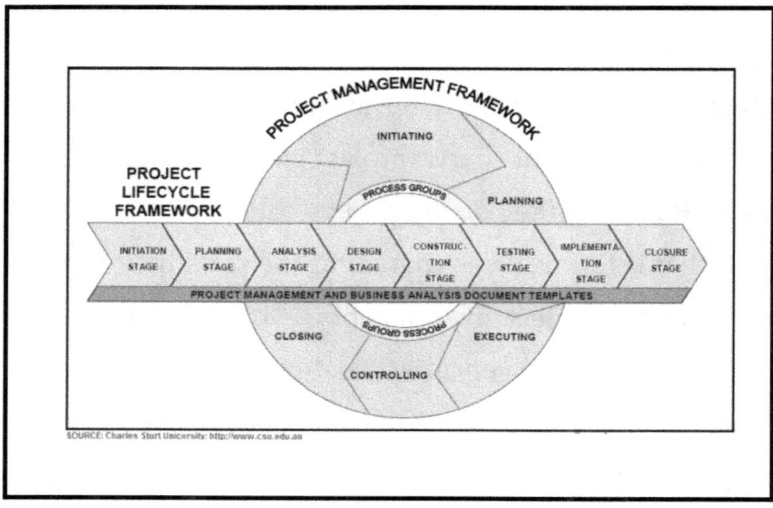

At this stage of our discussions, we will not explore the various components and sub-components of the project management framework in detail (more detailed discussions to follow). However, for now, it is important to

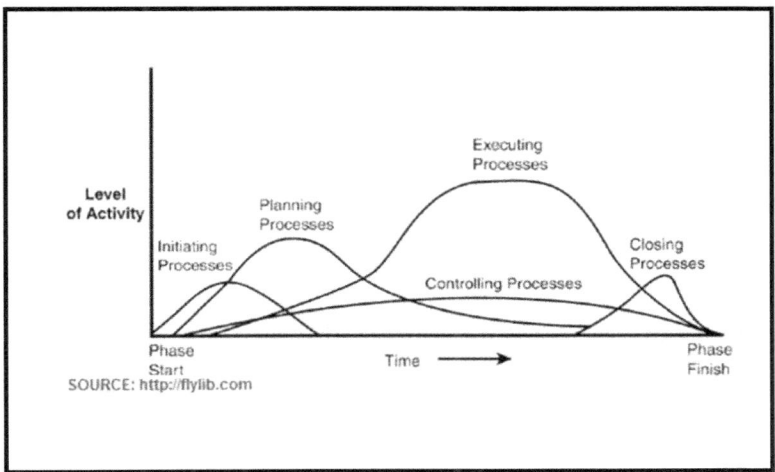

have a clear understanding of what the framework is. Viewed from a simplistic perspective, the framework sets out a blueprint for how to deliver successful projects. The lifecycle tells us how the project must evolve, in order to arrive at its end-state, while the Process Groups provide us a set of management tools that can be used throughout each stage of the lifecycle.

2.1 Introducing The Project Management Process

The act of managing projects occurs through the application of four (or 5, depending on how one views them) processes:

- Initiating
- Planning
- Executing
- Closing
- and an overarching Monitoring & Controlling process embedded within the above 4 processes

In order to adopt the best practices that the Project Management Body of Knowledge (PMBOK) espouses, aspiring (and veteran) PM's must understand that the project management process isn't entirely a set of discrete processes applied to a finite set of project phases (Stages). In fact, there are often overlaps within the two, since the "tools" (Processes within Process Groups) used are commonly applicable across Stages.

Simply put, the project management process is therefore an iterative set of specialised activities that are conducted throughout the lifecycle of a project. That's it! It is up to the PM (and his/her team) to decide which activities (processes) are applied to which Stage, and to what extent.

(See Chapter 4 for more detailed discussions on this subject)

2.2 Intro To Project Management Areas of Expertise

If PMs are to carry out the business of managing projects "...within the confines of a strong and robust framework", using a "...set of specialized activities", then they (PMs) must be equipped with certain expertise related to the said framework and processes. PMBOK delivers that expertise to PMs through a set of 9 Knowledge Areas (KAs).

These KAs include:

Integration, Scope, Time, Cost, Quality, HR, Communications, Risk and Procurement Management. Each of these 9 KA's contain sub-components, including inputs and outputs in the form of activities and artifacts, that PM's must plan, execute and manage over the life of the project.

A key point for PM's to remember is that these KA's are not always stand-alone, but often interact and integrate with each other. For instance, Procurement will have a high level of interaction with Costing, and potentially with Human Resources (for staffing).

(See Chapter 5 for more detailed discussions on this subject)

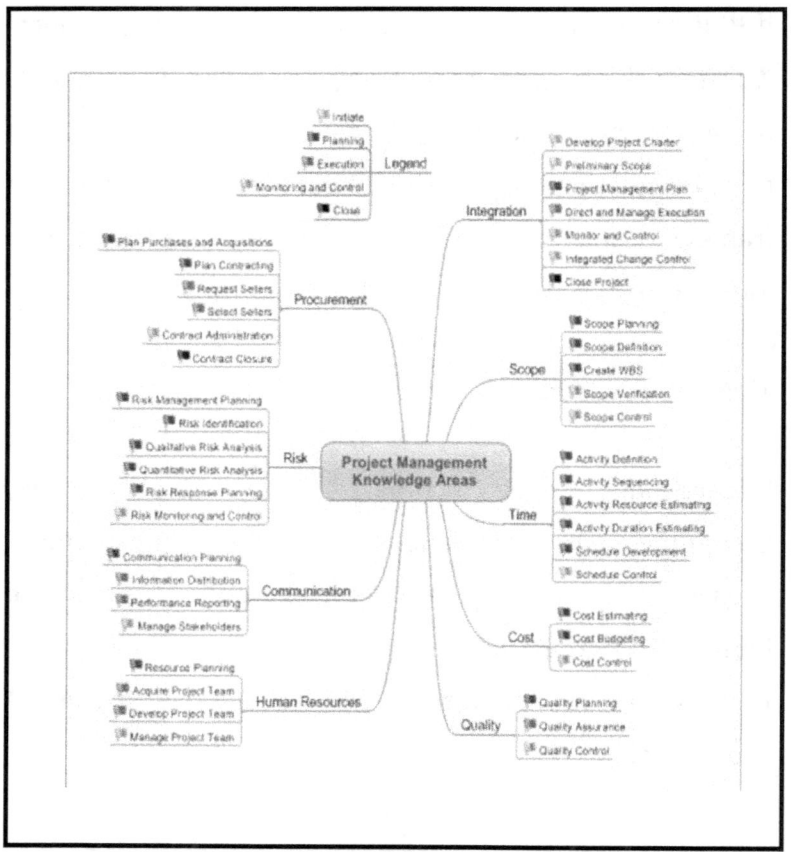

2.3 The Project Management System

In order for something as complex as project management to function effectively, it must operate within a disciplined and orderly environment. That environment is created by the PM using a "system". The Project Management System is a collection of methodologies, tools, processes, techniques, rules and norms used by each PM to manage his/her project.

Since every project, by definition, is unique, and the personalities, experience and knowledge of every PM is unique, Project Management Systems often tend to take on a unique flavour. Ultimately, adoption of the system will also vary depending on the type of organization within which the project is being managed.

Project-oriented organizations, which usually have PMO's, are inclined to adopt more formal project management systems. Other organizations, which only see projects as a means of producing one-off deliverables, may opt to keep their systems rather informal in nature. In either case, it is important for the PM to understand that his/her system must be able to adapt and adjust to the organizational environment - and not the other way around!

3.0 THE PROJECT LIFECYCLE

In Chapter 2.0, we introduced you briefly to the Project Lifecycle, and explained how the lifecycle fits within the overall project management framework. It's time to do a deeper-dive into the Project Lifecycle, and introduce you to each of the sub-phases.

We'll start by describing what the various stages of the lifecycle are, and discuss some of their features and characteristics. Next, we'll talk about the cost implications that PMs need to be aware viz. the lifecycle, and the impact that some stakeholder groups wield over the lifecycle of the project. Finally, we'll review how organizational maturity (defined as how "project friendly" or "project averse" an organization is) can impact the project lifecycle.

If you are an aspiring PM, your knowledge (or lack thereof!) of your projects' lifecycle, and factors influencing it, will greatly benefit (or hamper!) your ability to deliver a successful project outcome. It is with that fact in mind therefore, that you should pay special attention to the discussion to follow.

3.1   The Lifecycle Explored

Parents of children learn early on in parenting, that they must be aware of the various phases that their children will go through: From conception, birth, infancy, adolescence, pubescence, adulthood and old age, a parent does well to learn the "unique" needs of the child as he/she evolves. This same concept applies to project management.

Project Managers are akin to parents to a project. And by definition, a project evolves through its lifecycle, from vision to implementation, and faces changing needs throughout that lifecycle. It is those needs that a PM should be well aware of, and respond to, in order to ensure successful implementation.

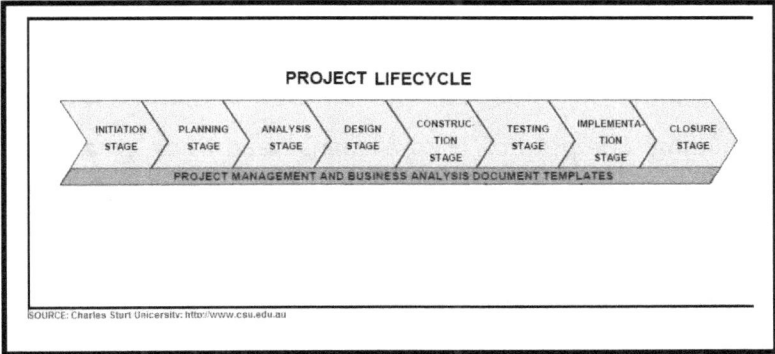

3.1.1　Initiation

This is where the vision of a project is first articulated. When the need for product or service is realized, project sponsors often initiate some form of due diligence to confirm:

- whether that need is real or simply perceived
- whether any (and what) solutions are available to deliver them
- whether delivering those solutions will result in favorable outcomes for the organization

There is some debate, amongst project management experts, whether this "visionary" stage should be included as part of the Initiation phase of the lifecycle, or whether it should be a project unto itself. Either way, a project must somehow be initiated, and the Initiation Stage has to occur at some point.

3.1.2   Planning

Once initiated, organizations do not immediately start "building" the project. Formal plans need to be created to take the project from vision to fruition. Failing to plan is the ideal recipe for disaster!

The Planning stage of the project provides project sponsors and stakeholders a clear blueprint of how the project will evolve from here on, what timelines will it need, what resources will be required, and what milestones will be accomplished on route to completion.

3.1.3   Execution

Here's where all of the relevant project activities are undertaken, to transform the plans into action. The Execution stage is further decomposed into sub-lifecycle stages:

- **Analysis:** Where detailed assessments of the problem to be addresses is conducted so that all relevant information, about the needs and proposed solution to those needs, is assimilated and analyzed. Following analysis of the situation, the project team comes up with the most optimal solution to the needs

- **Design:** Based on the proposed solution, the project team then designs suitable responses that can transform the proposed solution into reality. Often, the design phase may also include proof-co-concept (POC) mock builds of the proposed solution. However, the intent is often not to construct the solution, but simply to test the viability of the design

- **Build/Construction:** It is at this stage of the lifecycle that the project team starts the work of transforming the final design into the finished product or service

- **Testing:** As the solution is built, it is tested to ensure it performs as expected. Testing may be conducted in one go, once the solution is completely built, or it may occur in phases - gradually as each working component of the solution is built

- **Implementation:** Upon satisfactory conclusion of testing, the solution is ready for implementation.

This is where project stakeholders will see the return on their investment (ROI) in the project.

3.1.4 Monitoring and Controlling

Just as a child is continually nurtured, monitored, disciplined and controlled, so too the project lifecycle expects PMs to monitor and control each stage of the project, from Initiation to final Closeout. Failure to do so could lead to project's going over budget, beyond scope and surpassing planned timelines.

As with the Initiation stage, there is debate amongst project management experts as to whether the monitoring and controlling function rates a separate stage in the lifecycle. Regardless, whether separate or embedded, it does however occur at every stage of the projects' lifecycle.

3.1.5 Closure/Closeout

Unlike a home fence-painting job, real-world projects take a degree of formality to closeout. In addition to formal acceptance of the final solution, many a lose end needs to be tied up before the project team can be disbanded and return to "life before the project"

PMBOK packages all of these aspects of the Project Lifecycle into 5 Process Groups. We shall explore each of these Process Groups in greater detail in the next chapter.

3.2 Project Life Cycle Characteristics

Being aware of the Project Lifecycle will help PM's make many a crucial decision about how to manage the project. Decisions such as estimating project costs, securing project resources and assigning staff to execute on plans, will all be impacted by where the project is within its lifecycle.

It behooves the PM to understand some unique characteristics that define the lifecycle:

- The stages of the project lifecycle are usually sequential in nature, progressing from Initiation, Planning, Execution and Closeout in that order. This feature enables PM's to clearly demark boundaries for the project as it evolves over time
- In some circumstances however, especially where a project is extremely complex and long in duration, lifecycle stages may overlap for sub-components. For instance, Phase I of the project may be undergoing Implementation, while Phase II is still in the Planning stage

- Some sub-stages can be repetitive in nature, requiring project teams to perform them more than once during the lifecycle. For instance, if the Design turns out to be flawed, it may require additional Analysis. Similarly, if Testing fails, it may need additional Analysis, Design and Construction to be performed

- To be executed properly (using PMBOK best practices), each stage of the lifecycle must be initiated and closed-out formally. That means the creation of formal kick-off and conclusion procedures must be put in place

An intimate knowledge of where his/her project stands within the lifecycle, can give the PM valuable insights into how to manage the remaining stages successfully.

3.3   Project Cost Vs. Life Cycle

One of the biggest mistakes that aspiring and novice PM's make is around managing project costs. An intimate understanding of project costs as they relate to the lifecycle can easily help prevent such mistakes.

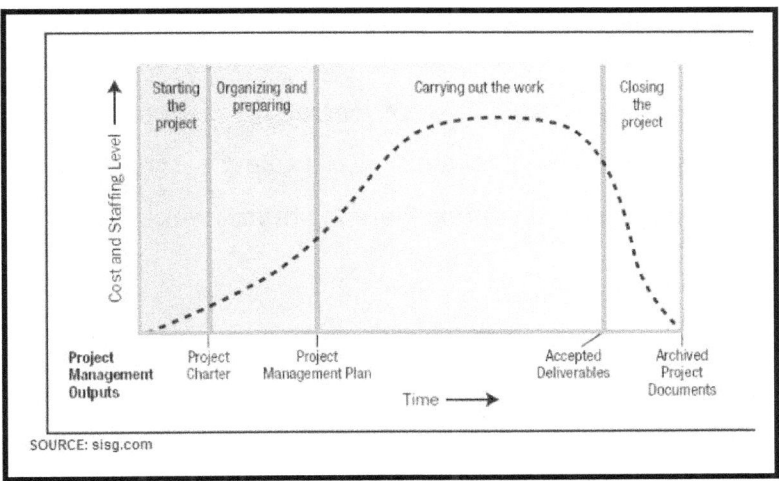

Unless there is something dramatically wrong with how the project is managed, project costs follow a predictable pattern:

- they are low when starting the project
- they rise when organizing and ramping up to execute the project
- they continue to peek, and ultimately plateau when carrying our project implementation
- they finally start to decline during project closeout

To be a successful cost controller, the PM must continually watch his/her budget with respect to where the project is within the lifecycle. If the project seems to be consuming more time, money or staffing resources than planned, it is less costly to take corrective action at the early stages of the lifecycle, as opposed to later.

As time passes, and the project moves into its successive lifecycle stages, the cost of corrective action starts to increase. Making changes to a project's scope is, for example, less costly during Planning than it would be during Execution.

3.4 Life Cycle Vs Stakeholder Relationship

Even though the PM "owns" the project budget, the relationship between projects and their stakeholders is such that the latter have tremendous influence over the cost of the project. This therefore leaves the PM vulnerable to stakeholder reactions to project deliverables. PM's need to understand what impact stakeholders have at various stages during a project's lifecycle in order to mitigate negative cost implications to the final outcome of the project.

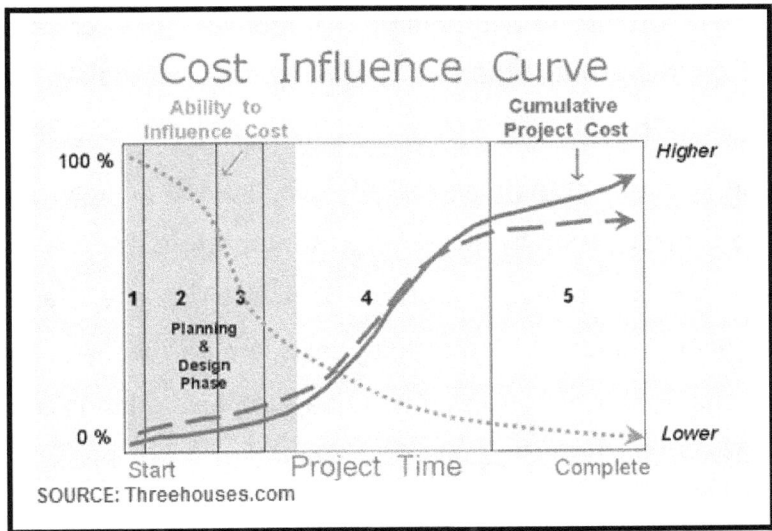

Typically, stakeholders have a greater ability to influence project deliverables and their costs at the beginning of a project. The PM must understand that it is the stakeholders who (usually) fund the project, and rather than building adversarial relationships with that group, he/she should forge a cooperative bond in order to avoid cost overruns and time delays in the project. Stakeholders can impact project costs by:

- Not participating fully during the requirement and scope definition stages
- Requesting (frequent) changes to project deliverables
- (Unduly) Withholding approvals of project milestones, thereby causing costly time delays to the project

The cost of entertaining stakeholder-dictated changes to the project generally increases as time progresses. It is in everyone's interest therefore, that project goals and objectives, and most importantly costs, are clarified as early in the lifecycle as possible. A harmonious relationship between the project team and stakeholders is the best way to achieve this.

3.5 Organizational structures and maturity Vs Project Lifecycle

Project teams are structured in various ways, depending on how "project-oriented" (or otherwise) an organization is. The more formal or hierarchical an organization is, the less autonomy a PM is likely to enjoy within a project environment.

In organizations, where there is a high-level of maturity about the role of projects, a Pure Project structure for project teams is preferred, while organizations with little to no appreciation of the role of projects usually prefer a Pure Functional structure for project delivery. A happy median is the Matrix structure. Pure Project organizations have well established processes to identify, initiate and execute projects; while Pure Functional orgs will offer little to no discretion to PM's when defining and running projects.

The PM usually does not have too much input into how the organization perceives the role of projects, as that is often a senior management decision. However, a PM's influence over the project lifecycle is the greatest in Pure Project environments, and less so in Pure Functional organizations.

Knowledge about organizational structures, and how projects are perceived and run, is extremely vital to the PM when building project teams, identifying project sponsors and establishing stakeholder relationships.

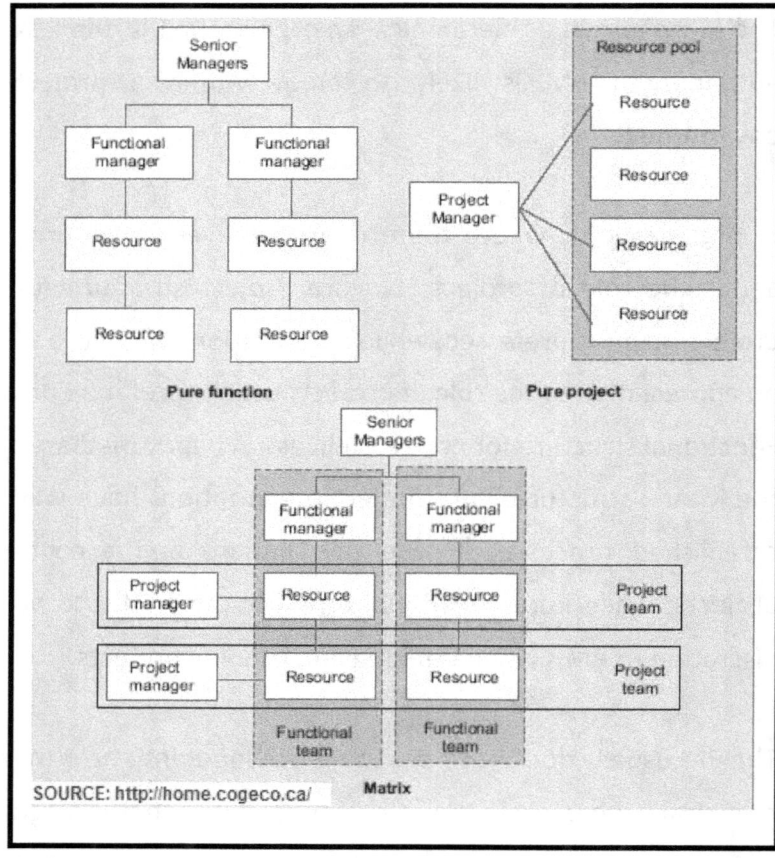

4.0 THE PROJECT MANAGEMENT PROCESS

In Chapter 2.0, we introduced you to the Project Management Process, within the context of the overall project management framework, and we also gave you a look into what the process entails, at a very high level. Back

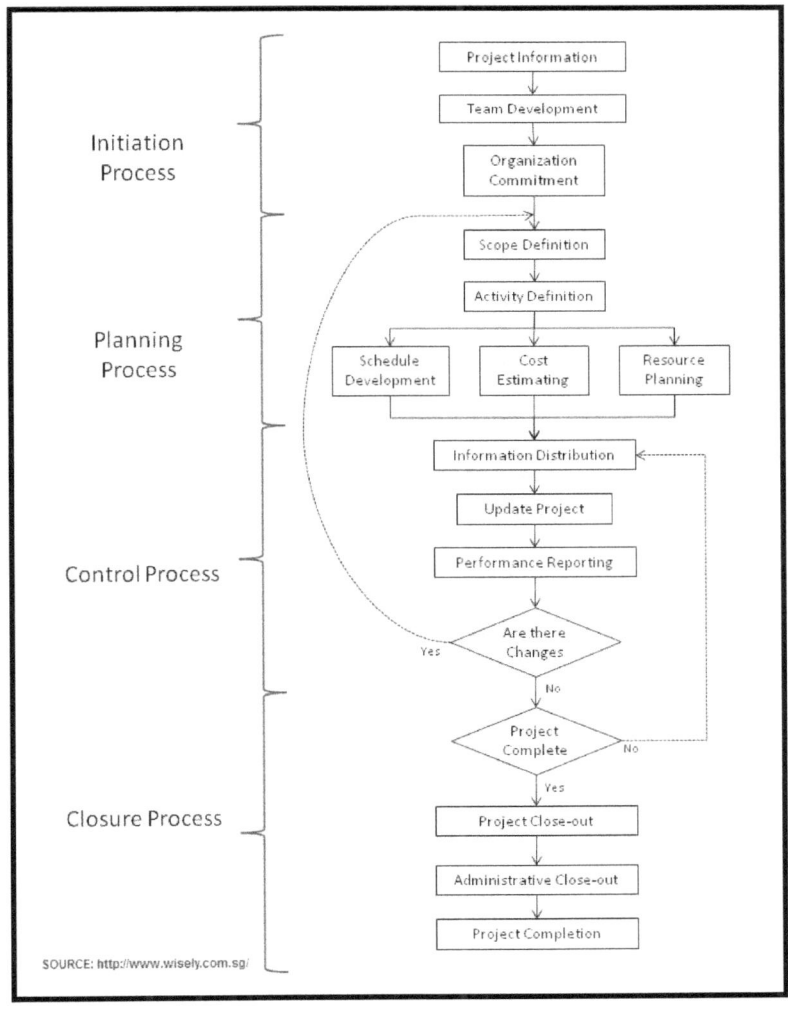

SOURCE: http://www.wisely.com.sg/

then, we promised you a more detailed look at the process later. And that's exactly what we'll do here.

Upon completing our more detailed review of the process cycle, we'll dive into the nuts and bolts of the 5 (or 4+1) Process Groups, and review the sub-processes within each of those groups. But first, let's set the stage for that discussion.

For theoretical purposes, project management is often presented as a set of discrete steps that have clear boundaries. However, seasoned PM's know that's not always the case.

The theoretical process is offered as a template, where the role of each of the project management processes (Initiation, Planning, Execution, Monitoring/Controlling and Closure), are defined for the PM to apply to real-life situations. It is then left to the PM to map those process elements to specific project activities. For instance, some PM's may wish to have "Organizational Commitment" confirmed even before the projects' Initiation process. Others would prefer to have a clear "Scope Definition" as part of "Initiation", and not wait until the Planning process to do so.

4.1 The Project Management Process Cycle

Looking at the Project Management Process in the context of individual activities, such as Team Development, Schedule Development or Communications and Information Distribution, does help us peg various activities to specific processes. However, it is more helpful if PM's start looking at those processes as a continuous "Process Cycle", instead of discrete stages or activities within the overall project lifecycle.

In that sense therefore, project management should be looked at as a repetitive process, and not a one-off series of activities conducted serially. For instance, the project Costing (budgeting) activity is not something a PM will perform just once - during the Planning process - but several times over the projects' lifecycle.

The American Society for Quality (ASQ) encourages the use

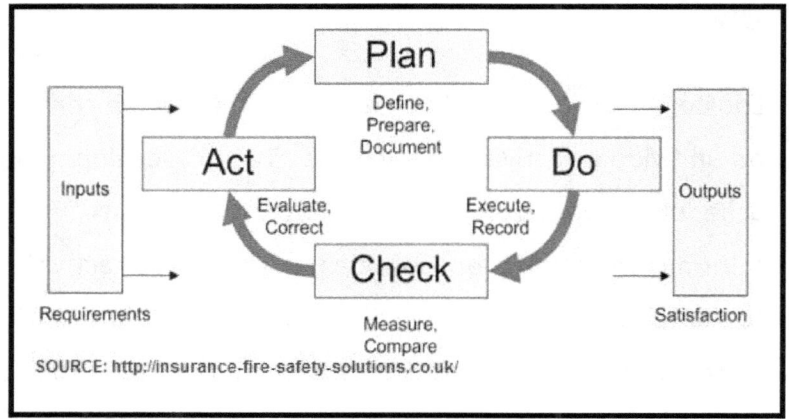

SOURCE: http://insurance-fire-safety-solutions.co.uk/

of the Plan-Do-Check-Act (PDCA) cycle, as advocated by noted quality management expert William Edwards Deming, to implement the project management processes as a continuous cycle.

Let's take the Planning Process as an example, and specifically the Costing/budgeting activity within it. Using the PDCA model, the PM might:

- Use the project Scope as an input to **Plan** the budget (during the Planning process)
- Spend budgeted amounts on resources, services, tools etc., while **Doing** various project-related activities during the Execution process
- **Check** to see if he/she is spending more than allocated during the Monitoring/controlling process

- **Act** quickly to ensure the excess spending is curtained by repeating the Planning process (revising Scope, Budgets, and Schedules etc.)
- Continue this cycle until all project deliverables are satisfactorily completed

The point being illustrated here, is that the project management process isn't necessarily linear in nature, but rather a circular one, where inputs (Initiation) of one process is used to drive (Execution) subsequent processes within the process cycle, until the project is complete (Closeout).

It's now time to take a deeper look at the 5 Process Groups and their sub-components.

4.2   The 5 Process Groups

Before we commence detailed discussions on the Process Groups, we should clearly understand that these 5 "groups" are distinct (and different) from the project Stages/Phases. Activities within the 5 Process Groups are performed across all stages/phases of the projects' lifecycle. And they are usually performed in a specific sequence:

- Initiating
- Planning

- Executing
- Monitoring/Controlling and
- Closing

When combined within the context of project stages/phases (Initiation, Planning, Analysis, Design, Build/Construction, Testing, Implementation and Closeout), it produces the framework within which projects are managed.

(See Chapter 2 for more detailed discussions on The Project Management Framework)

4.2.1   Initiation Process Group

As its name implies, the Initiation Process Group includes all the steps that will formally kick-off a new project or the next phase of an existing project. In most cases, the Initiation process will have been preceded by a "prequel" set of process, which would have recommended that the project should proceed. All of the information and artifacts prepared during the "prequel" processes should be leveraged and used as inputs for the Initiation process.

4.2.1.1 Develop Project Charter

The Develop Project Charter sub-process, of the Initiation process, will result in the creation of the Project Charter. This is a document which confirms the business justifications for proceeding with the project. In many ways, the Project Charter is a formal approval to the PM to use the organizations' resources to satisfy the business needs for which the project is being authorized.

4.2.1.2 Develop (Preliminary) Project Scope

The Project Scope is what sets out the boundaries of the project teams responsibility in greater detail than the Project Charter does. While the charter is used as a key input, the Project Scope document outlines elements such as:

- what specific deliverables are to be produced by the project
- how will the scope of those deliverables be identified, agreed upon and managed
- how will the deliverables be accepted and signed-off upon, and by whom

In other words, the Project Scope document spells out what the PM must deliver, and how he/she will know if it has been successfully delivered. It is important to understand that during the Initiation Process, it is only preliminary scoping that takes place. A more detailed scoping exercise will happen during the Planning Process.

4.2.2 Planning Process Group

The Planning Process Group's main objective is to develop the project plan, and other supporting plans, which will be used in the Execution Process. It is here too, that the project Scope is further refined in terms of specific work required to realize the Scope of work outlined during the initial Scoping exercise.

4.2.2.1 Develop The Project Management Plan

This process defines, prepares and integrates all the various sub-plans for the project, into a single Project Management Plan. The integrated plan is a comprehensive document which outlines how all aspects of the project will be planned, executed, monitored/controlled and ultimately closed out.

4.2.2.2 Planning and Defining The Projects' Scope

By now the PM is in possession of a high-level scope document, produced in the Initiation Process, which now needs to be refined into a scope planning artifact. It is during this process that the PM (and the Project Team) outline how the scope will be translated into a finite set of work activities, and how it (scope) will be managed and controlled, and how its completion will be verified.

The Project Scope document, which should be the end result of this process, will subsequently be used to validate project success, as well as to ensure that "scope creep" does not occur.

4.2.2.3 Creating The Work Breakdown Structures (WBS)

The Scope document will outline, in broad terms (but still in greater detail than what was scoped during Initiation), what the project needs to accomplish. However, it is the WBS process that will decompose those broad outlines and transform them into high-level milestones which, when delivered, will lead the project progressively towards completion.

4.2.2.4 Decomposing The WBS

It is now that the PM and the Team will develop a sequence of activities needed to accomplish specific project milestones, as well as work out estimates for the time and resources needed to complete them. The WBS will be decomposed into work packages, sub-packages, tasks and sub-tasks, each with their own resource requirements, duration and timelines.

A rule of thumb is to never wise to decompose a task more than necessary. Task-breakdowns should be done only to the extent that they can logically and easily be monitored and measured. Breaking down a 60-minute task into 5 sub-tasks will be counterproductive to the monitoring and controlling of that task.

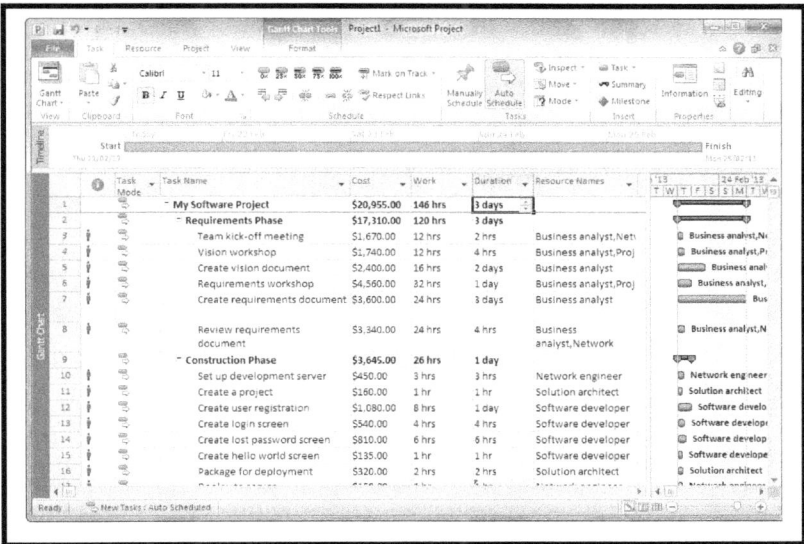

4.2.2.5 Developing The Baseline Schedule

Now that the PM has the "raw materials" (work requirements, resource requirements, duration and timelines) required for executing the project, he/she will start analyzing and sequencing all of this information in order to achieve the most optimal completion. It is during this process that constraints and conflicts will be discovered, and tasks scheduled (or rescheduled) to work within those constraints.

It is worth reiterating here that the Schedule, like all other project component plans, will continually be updated and revised throughout the project's lifecycle. Hence, this process delivers what's called a Baseline Schedule. Project progress is subsequently measured against this baseline to verify if slippage has occurred.

4.2.2.6 Costing (Budget Estimation)

With resource requirements and schedule in hand, the PM can now start putting together the approximate costs associated with all the scheduled project deliverables. This process will also define how the PM plans to manage, monitor and control project costs. Once the costing exercise has been conducted for individual work activities, the PM will aggregate all the identified costs and produce the Baseline Project Budget. Project costs are subsequently measured against this baseline to verify if over-spending has occurred.

4.2.2.7 Quality Planning

Over the course of the project, many deliverables will be produced. The Quality Planning processes will ensure that all relevant (and applicable) quality standards for those deliverables have been identified. The Quality Planning processes are also responsible for applying the selected standards and then monitoring them to ensure only deliverables of the highest standards are released for implementation.

An aspect of continuous quality improvement is central to this process where, if unsatisfactory performance is observed, immediate steps must be applied to correct the issues. The "defective" deliverables are then continued to be monitored until fully accepted by project stakeholders.

4.2.2.8 Human Resource Management (HRM) Planning

Most projects don't get delivered solely through the PM's efforts. It takes a team to deliver everything contained in the project Scope document. And like any other project resource, that team must be managed. The HRM processes are responsible for:

- Planning what roles are needed, and what their responsibilities will be. It also includes defining the various team reporting relationships for organizing the project team
- Acquiring and staffing all the roles identified
- Developing all of the skills needed to ensure the team has the capabilities to deliver committed project milestones
- Managing the team's performance, and resolving any inter/intra-team conflicts

HRM processes will involve elements of administrative work as well, such as maintaining and managing staffing records/databases, Time Sheet records, managing time and attendance records and implementing performance evaluation and rewards systems. Typically, such tasks are delegated to the PMO.

4.2.2.9 Communications Planning

George Bernard Shaw is famously quoted as saying:

> *"The single biggest problem in communication is the illusion that it has taken place."*

Some of the most challenging situations that PM's face, occur because they have no (or very poor) communications plans. Experience indicates that good communications can eliminate a significant number of project "issues" before they even become such.

In simple terms, the Communications Planning processes are designed to assess what each stakeholders' information needs are, and then make sure they receive that information per the format and frequency requested. It's that simple!

In real life however, managing that process can be a nightmare, and that's where the PM should properly plan his/her communications strategy in consultation with all stakeholders.

4.2.2.10   Risk Management Planning

No matter how "simple" a project is, there are always risks and threats to it - some visible, others hidden! The sooner that PMs realize that, the better.

Risk Management Planning processes are responsible for surveying the project landscape, internal and external, and identifying all possible risks (quantitative and qualitative) it faces. Then, after a thorough assessment, the PM (and his/her team) needs to put plans in place to respond to such risks, in the event that they arise.

PM's must understand that it is impossible to plan for all risk scenarios. Risk Management Planning is all about assessing the likelihood of a risk, and the severity of damage it might do to the project. Based on that assessment, a PM can either put plans in place to mitigate the risks, or make an informed decision to accept the consequences the risk carries.

4.2.2.11   Purchasing and Contract Planning

In most project environments, not all the products, services, resources and skills needed to complete the project are available in-house. The Purchasing and Contract Planning processes put in place various mechanisms to procure the lacking (missing) elements from outside sources.

PM's should be careful, not only of what to purchase, but in what quantities and when. The procurement/contracting plans must directly tie in with the overall project schedule.

4.2.2.12   Planning Done Right!

It is important for the PM to understand that the plans developed during the Planning Process, aren't what you may call "final". Throughout the lifecycle of the project, as new information about the project and its scope are discovered (uncovered), it will be necessary to revisit the Planning Process to varying degrees. Thus, the outputs of the Planning Process are never static - they are "living" artifacts that must constantly evolve and change.

4.2.3   Execution Process Group

Processes from the Execution Process Group are what will drive various activities needed to be performed to complete the project. In simple terms, the Execution Process uses all of the outputs created by the Planning Process Group, and executes them to deliver project requirements.

4.2.3.1 Managing the Execution Process

As a PM, one of your main responsibilities is to deliver what has been covered in the Project Scope. And the way to do so is to effectively manage the execution processes.

Execution is nothing more than following pre-defined plans as roadmaps. This requires putting in place all sub-processes needed to follow the plans (and sub-plans) developed through the Planning Process.

4.2.3.2 Implementing Quality Control

Meeting pre-defined quality standards is the primary goal when executing the projects' Quality Plans. These sub-processes include developing appropriate quality checking metrics, and putting in strong processes to detect, correct and validate any issues that may arise.

One crucial requirement of the Quality Control process must be to ensure that any changes made to project deliverables, due to quality issues, should not go beyond the originally defined project scope. A comprehensive Change Control process is therefore a cornerstone of the Quality Control sub-group.

4.2.3.3 HR Acquisition

Project execution depends on the availability of human resources, both in the desired quantity and quality. Therefore, the acquisition of staff to work on the project team is the primary goal of the HR Acquisition sub-process.

An important point for the PM to remember is that, how he/she staffs and manages the team will have a direct impact on the project's success. Factors such as internal vs. external teams and part-time versus full-time resources will be a prime factor in making HR acquisition decisions.

4.2.3.4 Team Building

More importantly however, is the impact of how the team is organized. Recall from our earlier discussions *(see section 3.5 for more details)* that organizational structures play a vital role in determining how a project team is constructed, and the level of influence a PM might have on the team. Part of the Team Building process' function is therefore to ensure that the PM organizes his/her team in keeping with the organizational culture and project management maturity models.

Building teams that are Functional in nature requires much more "politicking" than structuring a team using a Pure Project hierarchy. That's because functional project resources are not (usually) available full-time to the project, nor do they directly report to the PM. Managing such resources requires much more "savvy" than those that report directly to the PM.

Additionally, not all of the resources may come fully equipped with all the necessary skills. The Team Building exercise will need to identify the best approach to bridge those skills gaps in a cost-effective way.

4.2.3.5 Stakeholder Communications

Executing does not just mean "doing" what the project's scope requires. It also means making sure everyone who has a stake in the project knows what's happening and when. The Stakeholder communications process is responsible for reaching out to various parties-at-interest and share pre-defined information about the project with them.

The most important role of the Stakeholder Communications process is to engage stakeholders in advance, and ascertain their communications needs. Some groups are happy with receiving summarized information, others require more detailed updates. These requirements must be nailed down as part of the consultation process.

A usual point of conflict, between PM's and stakeholders, is not providing adequate notification during milestone events in the project's lifecycle. For instance, when major project deliverables are implemented, or when specifically requested changes are scheduled, these must be telegraphed well in advance so as to avoid conflict.

4.2.3.6 Seeking Vendors - RFQs, RFPs and RFIs

Executing on the project's Procurement Plan is what this process is all about. The process seeks offers from vendors, as and when the Project Schedule demands, to deliver goods and services needed, and determines if the offers should be accepted or rejected. Such offers will be solicited using Request For Quotes (RFQ) and Request For Purchase (RFP) sub-processes.

However, contrary to most beliefs, Seeking Vendors does not always (or only) have to result in a "buy" decision. The term "seeking" should also be interpreted by PM's as an act of scouring the vendor universe for potential partners who may subsequently be called upon (shortly, or in the longer term) to offer their products and services to the project. The Request For Information (RFI) sub-process is a fact-finding (or information gathering) process that makes the project team aware of potential future vendors and their solutions.

4.2.3.7 Vendor Selection

Once suitable vendors have offered their bids for the desired product, service or capability, the next step in executing the procurement plan is to select the appropriate vendor. The Vendor Selection process ensures that procurement plans are executed fairly and in accordance to the letter and spirit of the plan.

PM's must design the Vendor Selection process to not only rely upon the lowest price quotes offered, but also on the vendors track record and genuine ability to supply quality deliverables. Proposal Templates, Rating Metrics and Vendor Scoring techniques should be part of this process.

4.2.4 Monitoring & Control Process Group

While the Initiating, Planning and Execution processes are taking place, PMs need to keep watch over how each of them unfolds, and quickly take corrective action if he/she notices any deviations from plans. The Monitoring & Controlling Process group assists PM's in doing just that.

4.2.4.1 Keeping Track of Project Work

As project teams perform work on creating, delivering and implementing project deliverables, the PM is responsible for keeping careful track of such efforts. Recall that project work is conducted in line with carefully developed plans and schedules *(see section 4.2.2 for more on the Planning Process Group)*. A suitable process needs to be in place to gather details about actual work done, actual deliverables produced, and actual project budgets "burned", and to compare them against planned time and cost estimates.

Where discrepancies are noted, this process must apply corrective action, a function of the overarching Monitoring & Controlling sub-process we spoke earlier about, to bring the project back on track. *(Refer to section 3.1.4 and 4.2.4 for more on Monitoring & Controlling)*

4.2.4.2 Manage, Monitor & Control Changes (Change Control)

Savvy PM's realize that, no matter how well they may manage a project, changes will be requested by stakeholders - that's the nature of project management! The Change Control process deals with such events. It is necessary to have this process set up sp it can formally recognize the need for a change, acknowledge the request for it, and then receive formal approval to either accept or reject it.

Should the change be approved, the change management process then ensures the change is properly analyzed, scheduled, developed and rolled out into the live environment.

4.2.4.3 Manage, Monitor & Control "Scope creep"

Recall from earlier discussions *(see section 4.2.1.2 and 4.2.2.2 for more on the projects' scoping activities)* that project boundaries are clearly defined fairly early in the project management process. However, because there is often a significant lag between finalizing scope, and implementation, there is always a danger of the projects' approved scope expanding. There must therefore be an appropriate process to manage and control that from happening.

Veteran PMs will accept the fact that there will always be pressures (from management, project sponsors, clients and external stakeholders) to expand the scope of a project. Some of those requests may even be legitimate. However, the PM (of his/her own volition) is not authorized to use previously approved resources to satisfy such requests.

Any request that seems to expand the project's scope should be put through a formal process (review, approval, assess, schedule, develop, implement) that authorizes the PM to accommodate such requests. Where necessary, the PM may need to put such "Scope creep" requests through the Initiation, Planning and Execution phases of the project management cycle.

4.2.4.4 Manage, Monitor & Control Schedule Over-runs

The PM must put in place a formal process that continually monitors the project schedule *(see section 4.2.2.5 for more on the Project Schedule)*, and controls planned activity against actual results. Where significant schedule deviations are noticed, the PM may:

- formally request a change to the schedule to reflect the deviations
- add additional resources to the project to bring the schedule back on track
- re-schedule some (hereto serially planned) tasks to run in parallel to make up for lost time
- compress timelines for some down-stream activity to bring the project back on schedule

The process to Manage, Monitor and Control Schedule Over-runs will use data such as Time Sheets and Work Logs as inputs to track progress of work against plans. The frequency of reporting time spent, and the format in which this data is collected and processed, are some of the decisions that this process must address.

4.2.4.5 Manage, Monitor & Control Cost Over-runs

Every PM must also put in place an appropriate process, the Cost Control process, to Manage, Monitor and Control project costs. The process should ensure accurate and timely collection of project costs; the efficient review and analysis of such data, and its comparison against the projects' budget *(see section 4.2.2.6 for more on the Project Budgets)*.

Where significant cost deviations are noticed, the PM may:

- formally request a change to the budget to reflect the deviations
- reduce resources (temporarily or permanently) from the project to bring the costs back on track
- formally request change to the project's scope to account for project cost overruns

The cost control process will integrate closely with the project's Schedule Monitoring, Change Control and Scope Management processes, because information from those processes serve as an "early warning system" to PM's that costs might overrun.

4.2.4.6 Manage, Monitor & Control Quality

The Project Quality Management process is responsible for performing all activity related to ensuring only deliverables of the highest quality are produced by the project. This process therefore defines a Quality Plan, ensures the plan is implemented, and takes corrective action in the event quality standards are deviated from.

Since the term "quality" is often interpreted differently, the process to Manage, Monitor and Control Quality is responsible for:

- defining the parameters which determine "quality"
- agreeing upon metrics that will be tested to determine if quality parameters have been satisfied
- outline the process needed for quality to be accepted (signed-off) by the stakeholders

Two concepts that the PM must keep in mind are the concept of Quality Assurance versus Quality Control. Newly minted PM's often use these terms interchangeably. That is a mistake. "Assurance" relates to processes that ensure compliance with the Quality Plan *(see section 4.2.2.7 for more details)*, while "Control" is the function of processes that identify and eliminate deviations from the Quality Plan.

4.2.4.7 Manage, Monitor & Control Team Progress

In section 4.2.2.4 above, we touched upon the process to Manage, Monitor & Control Schedule over-runs. Such over-runs are a direct result of the pace of progress (or lack thereof) made by the project team in delivering agreed milestones. The team's progress depends on many factors, including work management and personality-related challenges.

The PM must therefore put into play a robust process that:

- ensures roles and responsibilities are well defined and clearly understood
- efficiently assigns and tracks work packages
- assesses work performance in a timely manner
- optimizes inter and intra-team dynamics
- identifies and removes all obstacles that hinder team performance
- takes immediate corrective action when team progress deviates from plans

It is a wise PM that manages his/her team through consensus rather than by decree. Regular team meetings and progress feedback loops are therefore vital to this process. Additionally, progress monitoring is not just about tracking and controlling a team's tasks, but also about monitoring and controlling others aspects of progress, including costs and scope.

4.2.4.8 Performance Monitoring & Reporting

Performance Monitoring and Reporting uses inputs from the Team Progress monitoring process, and is a function of several inter-related process, including Schedule Monitoring, Cost Monitoring, Scope Verification, Quality Monitoring and Procurement Monitoring. In short, the PM must initiate processes that monitor and measure all project activity against the project schedule, and report actual performance against the agreed performance metrics.

4.2.4.9 Stakeholder Management

How a PM manages and interacts with project stakeholder groups could ultimately determine the success (or lack thereof) of the project. Part of the Stakeholder Management process is to:

- understand the expectations of stakeholders; and then
- manage those expectations

A key element to that process is regular meetings with stakeholders, and frequent communications to update them on progress. Properly managed stakeholder relationships will result in each group of stakeholders receiving exactly what they need from the PM (information, updates, progress reports), to the degree of detail required.

4.2.4.10 Manage, Monitor & Control Risks

No project is immune to risks. Therefore, PM's must put in place a suitable process to Manage, Monitor and Control those risks. The Risk Management process should:

- take all risks - internal and external - into consideration
- assess the likelihood of those risks occurring
- analyze the impact to the project, should a risk be realized
- contain processes to proactively mitigate those risks
- have plans to deal with any risk that does materialize
- have contingency plans to accept any risks that the PM (or his/her team) cannot either mitigate or avoid

The Risk Management process is therefore not only about identifying risks, but also about moving forward with the project in the face of (known as well as unknown) risks that might materialize.

4.2.4.11   Management of Contracts

Many projects have heavy budgetary allocations to contracts. Such contracts can involve staff, materials, technology, tools or specialized capabilities. The Contract Management process is responsible to ensure that:

- the proper contracts are in place
- contract deliverables are properly accounted for (timing, quantity, quality)
- contracted deliverables perform as stipulated in the contract
- contracts are modified, extended or terminated in accordance to the Project Schedule and the Procurement Plan

Where contracts are managed by an organization's central contracting/procurement systems, PM's may need to "tweak" their individual project contract management systems to integrate seamlessly with organizational systems. If not, this could lead to unwanted confusion and conflict resulting in an impact to project performance.

4.2.5   Closeout Process Group

The Project Closeout Process Group is responsible to manage the orderly shut-down of a project. Whether a project was successful in delivering according to its scope, or if it is a premature (terminated) shut-down, it is essential that all of the closeout sub-processes be performed.

4.2.5.1 Closing Rites

The PM must prepare for eventual wind-down of the project. Closing Rites that must be planned for include:

- passing of all knowledge/expertise, for onward running/maintenance of the final deliverable (a product, service, facility, competence), from the project team to designated stakeholders/users
- ensuring orderly disbanding of project teams and formal reassignment (or dismissal, termination)
- accounting for all unused project resources (budgeted dollars, tools, materials, equipment, technology etc.), and returning them to authorized custodians

- winding down of all project-based capabilities (email accounts, access to company networks and services, facility access cards etc.)

The PM must ensure a formal process is put in place to receive sign-off, from authorized management representatives, that confirm he/she has performed all of these Closing Rites.

4.2.5.2 Close-out Contracts

Contracts with external sources are legal obligations, taken on by the organization on behalf of the project. They therefore merit special attention during project closeout. The Contract close-out process must be cognizant that some contracts may have clauses that grandfather those obligations well beyond the project's lifecycle (e.g. warranties, guarantees and service agreements). These situations must be dealt with appropriately during contract close-out process.

4.2.5.3 Documenting Lessons Learned

Projects don't just represent a huge investment in the final outcome (product, service or competency) delivered to the organization, but also in terms of the education and experience gained during the project. Part of the closeout process must also involve documenting all of the lessons learned, including:

- what worked
- what didn't work
- what should be done differently for the next project

There must be a formal process in place to document, review and accept the lessons learned document. The final version of the Lessons Learned should then be archived and made available to future PM's and project teams alike.

4.2.5.4 Management De-briefing

Management authorizes the project to kick-off, so they deserve to be de-briefed on the result and experiences from the project. The PM must have a formal process in place to deliver such a debriefing. The update must touch upon all aspects of the project, including:

- all stages, from Initiation to Closeout
- updates on budgets and timelines
- debriefing on scope and whether it was delivered (or otherwise - and why not!)
- feedback from the PM on organizational attitudes and reaction towards the project

A good starting point to prepare for this debriefing is the Project Lessons Learned document.

5.0 PROJECT MANAGEMENT KNOWLEDGE AREAS

Project Management can be viewed in two distinct dimensions. Firstly, as we've extensively covered in Chapter 4, it can be looked at in terms of a succession of processes, some of which are serially performed, while others are performed in iterative loops throughout the project's lifecycle.

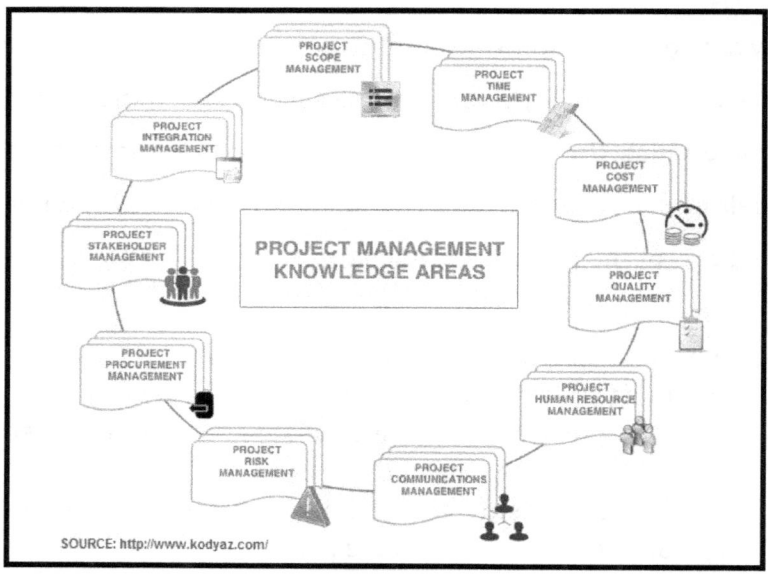

SOURCE: http://www.kodyaz.com/

Project Management can also be looked at as a series of "knowledge areas", which PM's must apply to manage the project throughout its lifecycle. Let's explore the 9 Knowledge Areas (KAs) that a PM should be familiar with.

5.1   Integration Management

Integration Management is the glue that binds all other Knowledge Areas (KAs) together in order to make the project run smoothly. Using skills in this KA, the PM kicks off the project, develops and executes upon the plan, monitors and controls various segments of the project, oversees the quality of project deliverables and finally, presides over project closeout.

Planning, coordinating and controlling are key skills tested in this particular KA.

5.2   Scope Management

"Scope creep" is the biggest nightmare of the PM. A project whose scope gets out of hand, is a project destined to fail. The PM's skills in Scope Management will ensure that the project is properly scoped, and that all on the team understand what that scope is. However, this KA also tests the PM's ability to manage changes (some valid, others not so much!) to the scope.

Key skills that this KA requires are negotiation, managing difficult situations and great communications and inter-personal skills.

5.3   Time Management

When it comes to projects, "time is money" is not just a cliché, but a reality! The Time Management KA deals with the PM's ability to sequence events and resources, and manage the overall project schedule. And as the project rolls on, the PM will also need skills to reign in time and schedule overruns, or manage scheduling conflicts.

It goes without saying, that the PM's time management abilities are crucial to this KA. However, this KA also requires good estimation and scheduling skills.

5.4   Cost Management

Just as a project can get out of hand from a schedule point of view, so too can it exceed its financial constraints and go over budget. The Cost Management KA helps the PM prepare an accurate cost estimate for the entire project, and then helps him/her monitor and control those costs.

The PM's ability to identify all major project costs (some are not so obvious!), and to estimate them accurately, are what's tested in this KA. The PM must not only have a good head for numbers, but should be a bold negotiator as well, especially when it comes to putting project contracts in place.

5.5   Quality Management

At the end of the day, a successfully completed project is all about delivering a quality project. The PM must be able to review the scope of the project, and determine what quality metrics should be applied to satisfy the projects' need for quality. Ignoring quality standards can lead to failure, but going overboard in the pursuit of quality can lead to time and cost overruns.

The PM should obviously have a flair for quality in order to demonstrate his/her command of this KA. And in doing so, he/she has to prove adept at both Quality Assurance (assuring quality standards are met) as well as Quality Control (controlling defects that may creep into a deliverable).

5.6   HR Management

HR management is a vast ocean, and many a PM has drowned while trying to swim it! This KA helps PM's define project roles and responsibilities, and then assists him/her in staffing, organizing and managing the project team.

Since human resources are a very "temperamental" commodity, the PM must possess exceptional "soft skills" -

motivation, communication, empathy, enthusiasm, passion - in order to demonstrate command of this KA.

5.7   Communications Management

It's been said that 60% of all project "issues" arise out of miscommunication. This KA supports the PM in communicating with the project team, with management as well as with internal and external stakeholders. But just communicating for the sake of communicating isn't sufficient for success. It must be substantive and timely!

To stay true to this KA, the PM must possess excellent verbal and written communications skills. Half of all communication is all about how the message is delivered, so he/she should also be a great presenter.

5.8   Risk Management

All projects face risks, and even people not trained in project management can often see them. The Risk Management KA however gives PM's the tools and capabilities to put in place formal strategies to identify, quantity, mitigate and accept those risks. As a result, PM's are also able to deal with unseen risk situations that often take others by surprise.

To excel in this KA, the PM should be plugged into not only the project environment, but also into organizational dynamics and external environments that might impact the project. Having strong networking skills can help the PM get forewarning of potential risks (from various quarters) long before they materialize.

5.9   Procurement Management

As someone responsible for arranging all the goods and services necessary to execute the project, the PM must be an adept Procurement Manager. This KA arms the PM with skills such as putting in place adequate procurement policies, preparing procurement packages, reviewing vendor responses and negotiating with vendors to get the most favourable terms for the project.

In addition to being well plugged into the sources of potential supply, for project goods and services, the PM must develop acceptable skills in the product/service being acquired. Strong negotiation skills and a fair degree of legal knowledge (pertaining to contract and tort law) might also come in handy.

SECTION III

This section will explore the practical aspects of Project Management. It is now time to move away from the theoretical discussions so far, into the more practical aspects of managing projects. When reviewing the contents of Section III, it is important for PMs to understand that the discussions below supplement, and do not replace, the theoretical discussions already held in previous sections of the book.

6.0 PROJECT MANAGEMENT IN ACTION

While talking about project management theory so far, we have stuck closely to the concepts and practices espoused by the PMBOK. PMs interested in pursuing formal Project Management designations will benefit greatly from those discussions. However, putting PMBOK into action isn't always "clear cut".

PMs must use their discretion and judgement in applying the Project Management principles discussed, to real life project environments. "Discretion", in this case, does not encourage radical departure from PMBOK, but it also does not mean a "literal" interpretation of its principles and practices. Real world projects will be successful if a happy medium is struck between theory and practice.

For instance, theory suggests the use of intricate quality control tools, such as:

- Cause and Effect Diagrams
- Control Charts
- Process Flow Charts
- Pareto Diagrams
- Run Charts and

- Scatter Diagrams

Many real-life projects might not require the use of such tools, or may work perfectly if customized versions of such tools are embraced. PM's must possess the knowledge to make those decisions. The object, of putting project management into action, is to make PMBOK fit to your project environment, and not the other way around!

The Process Groups (and their sub-processes), and the Knowledge Areas described in chapters 4 and 5, are meant to provide aspiring PM's an insight into how "typical" projects are planned, organized and managed, and what skills a "typical" PM needs to successfully manage them. When putting these aspects of project management into action however, PM's often have a great amount of latitude in defining the processes and using specific knowledge (skills) to manage them.

Peter F. Drucker, considered the father of modern-day Management studies, once said "What's measured improves". PMBOK recommends many measurement metrics that can help PM's monitor and control their projects. However, when putting project management theory into action, PM's must be careful which metrics to use, because not all available metrics may be practical or applicable to every project.

As long as PM's understand that, they will be extremely successful when putting into action everything outlined in this book.

7.0 PROJECT MANAGER SURVIVAL

So how does a PM take what's been explained in Section I and II, and put it into practice in the real world and survive. The answer is:

By using common sense to adapt theory to practice!

Project Management is as much of an art as it is a science. Here are some real-world tips and tricks that PMs can use to survive in the project management jungle:

- **Identify "power brokers" early - and align yourself with them:** It behoves a PM to align him/herself with people carrying the "big stick" in an organization. Actively look for them (during meetings, briefings, workshops etc) and you will find them

- **Don't over commit:** Promising something in 10 days (knowing it will really take only 8 days to complete) is a good strategy. If you are "delayed" by 2 days, you are still on schedule. If you deliver in 8 days, you're a hero!

- **Build contingencies in your plans:** Always have a Plan B in your pocket. You needn't disclose what those plans are to everyone. However, having them will allow you greater flexibility to maneuver if things go awry with Plan A!

- **Be careful about project reporting:** Once an idea or thought is published, it sets an expectation and often becomes into a "promise". Be careful how you word your reports and communications, least they become a nightmare for you later

- **"Over communication" really exists!** Strike a balance in your communications with stakeholders. Over communication can not only lead to desensitizing recipients to key messages, but sometimes it can cause cross communication and even miscommunication

- **Have your finger on the pulse at all times:** It is often impossible for the PM to know "exactly" what's going on in the project: Which team member is absent today; Who has clocked in early; How many tasks from a 50-task work package are being worked upon at any given time. Building a project dashboard, that provides you summary metrics, is a great way for you to maintain your finger on the pulse of the project at all times, without being inundated with the details

- **There is such a thing as "too many meetings"!** Meet only when necessary, and then too keep meeting durations to the minimum. Meeting too frequently or too long can be a drag on project teams

- **Document meetings - but focus on decisions/action plans:** A common mistake that novice PM's make is to have meetings copiously documented. While that may be important is some project settings, most projects are better served by simply documenting conclusions and action items

- **Delegate where possible:** For a PM to retain his/her sanity, delegation is absolutely essential. But how? When you understand that "delegation" does not = "abdication", you'll automatically learn to push down certain tasks to the team, while taking personal charge of others

- **Trust, but verify:** This is a corollary to delegation. When delegating, it is important for PM's to have mechanisms to verify that the task delegated was completed. This does not mean you don't trust the delegate. It simply means the buck stops with you (the PM), and you need to validate what you've delegated

- **Take time to motivate the team:** This aspect of Project Management is often ignored by new PM's. Just as a well maintained car performs at its peak, so to do well motivated teams perform at their best. Celebrating success is a great motivator. It must be encouraged at all levels

8.0   BEYOND PROJECT MANAGEMENT

The information provided in this book so far has been restricted to "projects", and how PM's should apply that information to manage them. However, in the real world, you are likely to come across a number of variations of a project, which we have not discussed here as yet, including:

- **Sub-projects:** When projects are large and extremely complex, management usually decides to break them down into smaller sub-projects in order to reduce risk and complexity.
- **Programs:** Entire initiatives, such as organizational IT Transformation, can sometimes be too broad in scope to group them into a single project. Management therefore sub-divides them into individual projects to maintain focus on specific aspects of the program. For Instance, the IT Transformation Program may include an Enterprise Software Transformation Project, a Mobile Communications Software Project, and an IT Infrastructure Transformation Project. Combined, these three projects will form a Program to transform the organizations IT capabilities.
- **Portfolios:** Organizations that are highly project-centric find it easier to manage their business as sets

of Portfolios. A combined group of Projects and Programs are managed together to enable effective management so that they can deliver on strategic business objectives. While most Programs comprise of dependant Projects (and sub-projects), Portfolios are not always made up of interdependent Programs.

The reason that these aspects of management are being introduced here is to highlight that project management is not an art and science with restricted capabilities. It stretches much beyond the traditional project environment.

The basic skills and knowledge required to manage all these three areas (Sub-projects, Programs and Portfolios) are the same. However, additional skills and expertise, especially around strategic thinking, vision building and leadership, are needed to manage Programs and Portfolios. The foundation however is laid through effective project management.

9.0 PROJECT MANAGEMENT - THE NEXT LEVEL

For those that aspire to take the next step into the Project Management world, and beyond, you should consider receiving formal training and certification. The information provided in this book so far provides a perfect segue to the discussion that follows.

There are a number of professional designations that project management enthusiasts can pursue. What follows is a list of a few such opportunities offered through the Project Management Institute, a professional body that oversees all such accreditation:

PMI's **Project Management Professional (PMP)**® credential is the most important industry-recognized certification for project managers. Globally recognized and demanded, the PMP® demonstrates that you have the experience, education and competency to lead and direct projects. This recognition is seen through increased marketability to employers and higher salary; according to the PMI Project Management Salary Survey–Eighth Edition, certification positively impacts project manager salaries.

Courtesy: **Project Management Institute**

PMI's **Certified Associate in Project Management (CAPM)**® is a valuable entry-level certification for project practitioners. Designed for those with little or no project experience, the CAPM® demonstrates your understanding of the fundamental knowledge, terminology and processes of effective project management. Whether you are new to project management, or already serving as a subject matter expert on project teams, the CAPM can get your career on the right path or take it to the next level.

Courtesy: Project Management Institute

PMI's **Program Management Professional (PgMP)**® credential recognizes the advanced experience and skill of program managers. Globally recognized and demanded, the PgMP® demonstrates your proven competency to oversee multiple, related projects and their resources to achieve strategic business goals.PgMP credential holders oversee the success of a program, grouping related projects together to realize organizational benefits not available if they were managed separately. It's the perfect fit if you define projects, assign project managers and oversee programs.

Courtesy: Project Management Institute

PMI's **Portfolio Management Professional (PfMP)**® credential recognizes the advanced experience and skill of portfolio managers. The PfMP® demonstrates your proven ability in the coordinated management of one or more portfolios to achieve organizational objectives. PfMP credential holders are responsible for the execution of the portfolio management process, communication around portfolio progress, and recommendations for action. Where project and program managers are responsible for "doing work right," this is an ideal credential if you are responsible for ensuring your organization is "doing the right work."

Courtesy: Project Management Institute

If you are ready to take the plunge, this book is ideal to get you started. You can then find many FREE online resources that can provide you additional insight into the specific certification you wish to pursue. Your next step should be to seek out reputable Registered Education Providers (REPs) to take you to the next level. Good luck!

10.0 USEFUL PROJECT MANAGER TOOLS & LINKS

1) Find a REP near you

2) Looking for advanced Project, Program and Portfolio Management Standards, Guides and Toolkits?

3) Want an app to simplify your project bug and issue tracking process?

4) Want a tool that allows you to share project files, hold discussions, work collaboratively on project artifacts, assign tasks, and check due dates?

5) Looking for a way to get your project team to actively collaborate when managing and executing projects?

6) If you want to keep accurate track of project-related time and costs, then this may be of help!

7) Learn the basics of Microsoft Project - the tool that every PM should know how to use!

8) Want a FREE Trial for the PM's "must have" tool - Microsoft Project?

9) Use this link to test your knowledge about some of the topics discussed in this book

10) If you want to hone your PMBOK knowledge before taking a PMP exam, you may find these mock tests a handy exam prep resource

Now that you have an introduction to formal Project Management, you might want to hop on to the latest innovation of the Agile Methodology called Scrum.

Free Preview – Scrum, Your Quick Start Guide to Adopting Scrum For Your Organization

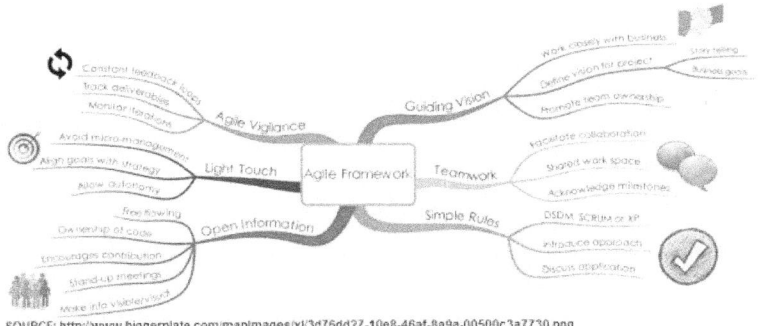

SOURCE: http://www.biggerplate.com/mapimages/xl/3d76dd27-10e8-46af-8a9a-00500c3a7730.png

In order to be an effective tool for its adherents, any body of knowledge needs a formal framework within which to function. Agile is no exception. Agile methodologies like Scrum {and others, like Dynamic System Development Methodology (DSDM) or Extreme Programming (XP)}, work within a framework that governs how the various tenants of the Agile body of knowledge should be applied to project management.

Unlike Waterfall, which stipulates that the project be run as distinct phases, with deliverables (either final or interim) being produced at the end of the project, Agile instead prescribes a set of conventions that project managers can then adapt when delivering projects. Hallmarks of the Agile Framework include:

Agile Vigilance: Which stresses the need to build feedback loops within the project that continually monitor and track all aspects of the project, and to adapt themselves to the project's dynamic environment

Light Touch: Which encourages a much higher degree of project team autonomy than Waterfall does. Project teams move away from an environment of strictly imposed order, and gravitate into self-managed structures

Open Information: This enables the free flow of information and views between all stakeholders on the project. This allows the team to assess changing conditions and quickly adapt their responses accordingly

Guiding Vision: The objective here is to facilitate behavioural changes that ultimately result in internal and external stakeholders working to achieve a common goal.

The vision is shared by everyone, and so it influences positive outcomes, which leads to project success

Collaboration & Teamwork: This part of the framework is meant to promote healthy interactions between teams, and encourage cooperation amongst everyone in order to meet the desired goals

Simple Rules: The Agile Framework recognizes that a simple set of guiding principles (rules) can often be used to support extremely complex environments, including interactions and relationships amongst team members. The more

---

Good to know:

A rugby scrum restarts a rugby game after a minor infringement of the rules. Understand what goes on. Who puts in? How do you win?

Definition of a "Scrum" - Rugby Sidestep

---

complex these rules get, the greater chances of misunderstandings that lead to project failure

Using this framework, Agile methodologies like Scrum are able to manage projects that function in dynamically changing environments, and which can respond quickly to the changing functional demands of their stakeholders.

2.2 What Is Scrum?

Literally speaking, the word "Scrum" is an adaption of the work "scrummage", and denotes a situation of confusion and chaos. The term "Scrum" has its roots in the sports world.

If you are a Rugby fan, you'll often witness scenes like that depicted by the picture here. That, essentially, is what a scrum looks like out on the Rugby field.

Readers of a book on Project Management might well ask "So, what's Rugby got to do with the project management methodology"? Lot's actually, since the

methodology owes its origins to the Rugby playing fields. That concept of Rugby players "Scrumming" and regrouping to start off an interruption in play, has been taken and adapted by project management experts, and applied to the world of managing projects.

2.2.1 Scrum In The Project World

In order to win, sports teams need to be nimble, just as project teams must be agile to be successful. When we look

---

Good to know:

A Scrum is a way for teams to work together to develop a product. Product development, using Scrum, occurs in small pieces, with each piece building upon previously created pieces. Building products one small piece at a time encourages creativity and enables teams to respond to feedback and change, to build exactly and only what is needed.

Definition of "agile" Scrum - Scrum.org

---

at how "typical" projects work, we see striking similarities to the sports world. Individuals (Players) form groups (Teams) and work on specific tasks (Plays) to deliver successfully (Win) on commitments made to stakeholders (Fans). Periodically, there are frictions (Infringements) amongst individuals and groups, and project members have to regroup (Scrummage) to sort things out.

Management experts took all of those similarities, wrapped them around a proven body of project management knowledge, and created an agile approach to managing and delivering projects, which they called "Scrum".

In developing the Scrum methodology, experts realized that there needed to be a certain discipline behind the science of project management. What they discovered is that projects can consistently be delivered to spec, on time and within budget, if PMs:

- Organize the business into smaller self-governing, cross-functional teams;
- Organize work into smaller chunks of deliverables;
- Rank, prioritize and estimate completion and delivery;
- Organize delivery of small "working components" into shorter fixed-timeframe (1 to 4 week) Iterations (or "Sprints")
- Consult with customers/end users and organize release plans based on inspection results of each iteration
- Optimize the entire process based on retrospective review following every iteration

This is the central idea from which Scrum evolved.

2.3 The Scrum Framework

Delivering a project in accordance with the requirements of various stakeholders is an inherently challenging task.

However, Scrum has made that challenge easier to navigate by prescribing a "framework" for conducting the project management process.

The Scrum framework revolves around some basic "Scrum values" that practitioners must adhere to, including:

- Commitment
- Openness
- Focus
- Courage and
- Respect

Within these value parameters, complex projects can be delivered through collaboration and effective teamwork. The main focus of successful Scrum is to try and effectively manage a Product Backlog of deliverables that represent the "whole". This, in turn, is done by breaking up the "whole" into smaller deliverable backlogs known as Sprint Backlog. As each Sprint is completed, it adds value to the deliverables produced by previous Sprints, so that the final Sprint marks the culmination of the project.

To read the whole book, get it on Amazon by following the link below:

http://www.amazon.com/Scrum-Quick-Start-Adopting-Organization-ebook/dp/B00SRSVW22

www.ingramcontent.com/pod-product-compliance
Lightning Source LLC
Chambersburg PA
CBHW070907180526
45168CB00005B/1962

* 9 7 8 1 5 0 8 5 9 9 4 6 3 *